Poems and random thoughts

Working

While I am at work I get lost in thought
I think about all of the bad things
I think about all of the good things
I walk around and make my lists
I walk around and order the rest
I wait for customers
I hear drinks being made
Dishes are brought down, but no food is ordered
I talk to my coworkers
We have discussions
I can slowly feel my anger rising
Why?
I am being disrespected
I am being told things that are rude
I am told that I am too young to know
I am too young to do things right
I am too young to have the pain I do
I am too young to be given an important position
So I ask
Do you know me?
Do you know what I have been through?
Do you know why the bosses trust me more than you?
Do you know why I am angry with you?
They look at me and shake there head
We don't speak the same languages
We have a hard time understanding each other
But still she should respect me
I deserve to be respected
I fought long and hard for my position
I am one of the best at what I do

So why is it that just because someone is older
They don't have to respect the younger ones?
They don't have to listen to the person in charge?
They can do as they please and wont be reprimanded
But as soon as a guest complains, its my fault
even though I have repeated myself 130 times and was ignored
Is it still my fault?
Am I really the one to blame?
Is this how life goes or am I being punned?

Herstellung und Verlag: BoD – Books on Demand,
Norderstedt
ISBN: 9783756213078

Killing

Why is it that for normal people killing is illegal but for soldiers its okay?
why make the soldiers kill innocent lives?
why pay them as if saying their deeds are fine?
We as people have been brainwashed into believing that Its all fine as long as its for the causes of war
we have been taught that our government is right and not question them
They will tell you its for the greater good
they will tell you that they were our enemies
they will tell you that its for our sake
they will tell you that it will benefit everyone in the long run
they will tell you its part of the soldiers job
but here is the truth they hide from everyone
Those soldiers don't always return
those soldiers who do return aren't always healthy
some lost limbs
others lost their minds
some lose their families and homes
others cant find a job afterwards
then they are abandoned by the very people they protected
and as you lay in the night having peaceful dreams
A soldier has taken his life because the nightmares and demons have beat them down so much they cant take it
so before you disrespect the uniform or person in it, remember you know nothing of the pain they go through
you don't know what they have seen or have to remember every time they close their eyes
we don't see their pain
we don't see what happened to them
we have no clue as to what really happened
and that is why we as a people are part of the problem
we don't help them
we rather look away then see what the actual problem is

we rather pretend that nothing is wrong
we rather tear down the very people who we thank our lives for then help
that's why the people will forever be the problem

Boredom

As I stand and wait for something to do
I think of different things
some things are nice
others disturbing
I talk to my coworkers
I talk to my bosses
I listen to music
I write poems and stories
I try to occupy my mind before I go insane
Dark thoughts enter my mind
I look at my colleague
I start to tell her about these thoughts
she looks at me scared
she then looks away
I start to slowly see that my demon is coming out
that's when I decide to write it down
as a way to torture my colleagues and my poor but equally disturbed readers
So that they may indulge in the madness that is my mind

The thoughts that keep me up at night

Why do humans lie?
why do they feel the need to hurt others but not heal them?
why do humans tear each other down so easily but have no idea on how to build them up?
why are we told as children that lying isn't okay but as an adult its normal?
why do humans always make the same mistakes yet feel no need to change or learn from them?
why do humans always feel its okay to be rude and mean but find no need in being nice or caring?
why tell some they will be going to hell even though they don't know them?
what is the point of living in a world where no one cares and happiness is measured by the amount of money you make?
why keep trying when everything is pointless?
what is the true meaning of life and love?
why can humans never be happy?
why must they destroy everything without thinking twice, and when they do they don't realize its already too late?

Restaurant worker

We smile all day
we exhaust ourselves if it makes our customers happy
We deal with many rude and mean people all day
we get paid for less then we deserve
and for what?
To do it all over again
to go into work the next day only to be called names and told we are too stupid for an actual job
what they don't know is that here you actually have to go to trade school for these jobs
you actually have to pass a test after learning for 3 years
some do this job because they love it
others had no other open options at the time
some still do it because they still find joy in small moments
I do it because, people come to me in need
I do it for the little money I get
I do it for the small moments where someone smiles and tells me it was delicious
I do it for my Bosses you need me
If not for those reasons I would have quit before I even did my test
so for those of you who don't believe in giving tips, Remember......
without us you would have to cook, clean, and get your own food
without us you would have to go buy food, and drinks and carry it around alone
to you we may not seem busy or intelligent
but a lot goes into running a restaurant
all in all people should be more grateful for us who strive to make things easier for you by doing these humble jobs

Since when?

Since when is it okay to tell someone they cant eat at certain places
because of their size?
Since when is it okay to tell someone not to drink certain things
because they are fat?
since when do we publicly shame someone just because they are a
stranger?
since when has it become okay to be rude and obnoxious to people
we have never seen or met before in our lives?
has no one ever taught them to treat others as they want to be
treated?
has no one ever told them that if they cant say something nice, then
they shouldn't say anything at all?
Were they not taught to be kind?
were they not taught to be understanding?
were they not taught to never judge someone?
Since when did we start teaching children that its okay to be a
bully?
since when did we start standing by and watching instead of
helping?
since when did we start thinking its okay to let others be bullied?
when will things change?
when will they get better?
how long will we let this continue?
how many more young people do we have to let die before we fully
understand and change things?
How much more must we endure the pressures of those around us
until we decide we will be the ones to change everything?
how much longer will you stand still?
how much longer will you not do anything?
Its time we stand up and do something against these bullies
we have to be the starting point
otherwise nothing will ever change

War

Why are wars started?
Why do they keep going?
why must we kill innocent souls?
Why build more weapons instead of make solutions?
Why make matters worse?
Why not ask and give the people what they want?
Instead of war, why not peace?
This planet doesn't need any more wars or bloodshed
It would be a much nicer place to live if we would stand together instead of against each other
Children could go to school and play without a care in the world, as it should be
It would be better if children wouldn't know what true pain is
but since adults make rules and start fights and wars
children's pure souls become black with sadness and pain
they slowly start to see what the world is truly like
thcy losc sight of the light
they lose their pureness and become souls in which can no longer be saved
and why?
because they say their families get killed
because wars break out
because adults see an opportunity and kidnap and sell the children
because no one cares anymore
because the world has become a dark place in which their is no saving
and as adults instead of saving these children we let it happen
its far away from us so it doesn't concern us
but what we fail to realize is that its happening in our own backyard
and when we do realize it.....
Its too late

What I long for as an adult

As the days grow longer and the cold air shifts to warm
I think of the days where I was young
I think of the 3 months where I stayed home
I think of the warm days
I think of the thunderstorms
I think of the dangerous weather
I think of the fun times
I remember the stench from the cattle as we drove by
Sometimes I miss those days
I miss being a naive child
I miss staying at home and doing nothing
I miss the road trips
I miss not having a worry or care in the world
I miss not having to think about my job
I miss not having to worry about money
I miss not having to make my family proud
I didn't have to watch what I said
I didn't have to watch how I act
I didn't have to worry about how I look
I could goof off if I wanted
I could have a lazy day
I could do as I please
As long as the chores were done
as long as the house was clean
as long as my grades were good
I could do anything I wanted
I could be who I wished
I could have fun as I wished
That's what I miss the most about being a child
As an adult you learn that though life may suck
and life my use a grenade launcher to throw lemons into your face
you deal with it
you learn to take it as it comes, deal with it, and move on

so in a world full of adults don't let your inner child die
learn to live your life to the fullest
even if it means that you look like a fool
only those who are truly pure at heart will befriend you
so don't let your childhood days come to pass
make them apart of your adult life and never give up

Everyday

Make the most of today
You never know when it will be your last
and as you stand at the gates of hell
can you truly say you lived a good life?
You should make the most of the time you have
go out, do good deeds, be yourself
be kind to others
have fun
don't listen to people who are ignorant of who you are or who you
want to be
make choices that you deem fit
don't let others tell you what you need to do
We go our entire lives following others
But why?
who told us that we need to follow like lambs?
we were all meant to be alphas
somewhere along the way between childhood and adulthood We
learn to follow and not lead
It is up to us to define who we are
because on our judgment day, we stand alone
so I believe we must live everyday as though its judgment day
for we are our own people
we must change ourselves in order to change our world
so instead of being mean and rude
instead of following trends
instead of following popular beliefs and lifestyles
find what is best for you
stand firm
and be yourself
even if the entire world stands against you
for there may be one person who wishes to walk your path with
you
and that one will stand with you against the world

or might want to protect you
so don't give up, be yourself, and fight

Random thoughts in dark times

As we sit and wait to play our simple game
we talk and eat all the same
we have some fun and drink our favorite things
we laugh and joke and continue to wait
we watch the adults and all the children
we realize how good we actually have it
we realize in all the bad that's going on
We have much more that's good
as the night turns to day, and another 100 leave us
we keep up with our daily lives as not to lose faith
we goof off and pretend not to see
we pretend to show we aren't scared
we pretend to be ignorant of the war happening
But in actuality we see
we hear
we acknowledge everything
we know of the death rates that are rising
we know of the war that wages on
we know of the children and mothers who cry in the night
but we cant help everyone
we cant save the world
we can only do so much
that is why we continue on as if nothing is happening
because if we truly see and hear all the bad

it becomes a crippling depression that makes us mad
and as we lay at night to sleep
the thought comes up of what may come to be
If the war keeps on we may have to fight too
and many become scared and start to act irrationally
as a person who wishes for peace
I too am worried of what may be
I look at the sky and pray
that peace be near and not death

Where are you?

as day turns to night I think of you
I wonder where you are
I wonder what you are doing
I wonder why you never talk to me anymore
I wonder what it is I did to make you hate me
I think of the days we use to talk non stop
I think of when we went to school together
I think of the times we laughed
I think of the times we cried
I think of all the times you helped me
I think of all the times I came running to your side when you needed me
I think of all the things we did
I think of all our memories
I slowly start to wonder if you are even still alive
Did you leave this planet?
why wasn't I told?
Did I do something wrong?
Did I ever tell you I love you?
Would you have even given me a chance to love you?
where did things go wrong?
If I could change the past the one thing I would change is our friendship
I would want you as my girlfriend and not just a friend
I would take you on actual dates
I would buy you flowers
I would buy you chocolate
I would tell you daily I love you
We would move to Germany together
we would have started our pet family
And maybe someday get married and adopt children
we would then grow old together while sitting on a porch drinking sweet tea and reminiscing old times

then we would die together
and would be together in our next lives
but because I don't know where you are
and because I never told you what I should have
we are far apart and will never see each other again
so as someone who was a coward
I cant even tell you I miss you and will always love you
I will forever keep you in my heart
I will forever wish for the best for you

Wondering mind

As I lie awake in my bead, I think of many things
I wonder what my next life will be like
I wonder if I will have to always work as hard as I do
I wonder if I will forever have to suffer
I wonder how much longer I have
I wonder when will there finally be peace
We live in a world that is moving ever so faster but no one seems to notice
We live out our days doing the same things over and over
nothing ever changes
We refuse to see what is truly going on
we refuse to see what is wrong
we refuse to hear the cries of help
we refuse to change ourselves for the better good
and why?
because we are told nothing is wrong
because we are told to follow and keep our heads down
and as I lie awake at night, letting my mind wonder
I think of all those who cant sleep in a warm bed
I think of all those who are in constant fear
I think of those who are on deaths door
I think of those who cry themselves to sleep
I think of everyone who lost someone today
I think of all those who are also just lying there waiting for morning to come
and as I leave my house, wishing it would be a great day
I am reminded that no one thinks of others
I am reminded that no one is kind
I am reminded how dirty the world has become
I am reminded of how evil has taken over the hearts of many people
And as I go to work or go home I am again reminded of how alone I am

No one thinks like I do nor will they ever
I get home and greet the solitude that has become the norm
I acknowledge the fact that I can never truly be loved
I am not saddened by this
nor do I care about how others perceive me
I only wish for true peace on earth
But since humans are incapable of loving others
since they cant learn from past mistakes
There will never truly be peace on earth

Short ride home

As I sit on the bus and listen to drunken blabbering
I think to myself why this is normal
You and your friends are beyond drunk
Most will probably fall asleep soon
And yet you talk about partying more?
How?
With what money?
You'll throw up, and that's a waste of good liquor and money
So why keep going?
Don't you know when to call it quits?
Is this really the norm?
Why do humans do this?
Why act like this?
What's wrong with everyone?
These are the moment where I understand humans less than ever before
Must this go on?
When will they realize their mistake in doing and acting like this or am I the only one?

Random thoughts of love

You are the moon
I am but a lonely star
I watch as you move
I watch as you smile
I keep my distance
I hope one day you will notice me
But alas
You will never look my way
For as I watch you, you look at someone else
You smile at them
you wave at them
You are happy with them
But as I watch you, and remain in the darkness
I also see the other
I see that he doesn't look at you the way I do
I see him looking at others, but whispering love in your ear
I see what he is, but since you love him I dont bother
Because I know......
No matter how much you love someone, they wont always love you back
I also know that I can protect you
and that is what I do
so whenever you do get hurt, you can always count on me
I will be your shoulder
I will be your light in the dark hours
I will help you find your way
I will always be waiting for you
because no matter what
my love for you will always be stronger than anyone elses
So I will wait patiently until you can love me too

Whats the cost?

It costs nothing to be kind
It costs nothing to be nice
It costs nothing to stand for the old
It costs nothing to stand up for what you believe in
So why does everyone find it so hard to be a decent human being?
Why do so many forget their manners?
Why is it that the Golden rule no longer applies to Adults and isn't taught anymore?
Why is it that treating others with Respect isn't a given anymore?
I wish things would go back to how they should be
I wish that everyone on earth could be friends
I wish everyone could get along without being prejudice
I wish racism didn't exist
I wish it wouldn't be taught
That is why we need to tell children not to be that way
That its okay to be friends with everyone
That nothing actually matters when making friends or when it comes to love
only then will we have peace on earth
only then will things go back to how they were
only then will children stop dying for stupid reasons
only then will the world finally have a day where no one dies

Birthdays

Why do we stop celebrating birthdays after becoming an adult?
as children we celebrate every year until the age of 18 and then we stop
but why?
Is it because we become afraid of age?
Is it because people stop caring?
Is it because we find it no longer necessary?
I believe we should celebrate not only every year, but also everyday
we never know what can happen tomorrow
You could die tomorrow
you could lose a dear friend
you could lose family members
anything could happen in the blink of an eye
that's why you should celebrate living
and even if someone you love dies
you should celebrate their life
and you should celebrate their death
because even in death they stay beside you
so go out
have fun
celebrate
and forever and always be true to who you are

New beginnings

As most know Spring is meant as a sign
It is a sign of rebirth
It is a sign of new beginnings
It is a sign of new things to come
We can recreate who we are
we can change the things we do not like about ourselves
We can become someone better
we can change jobs and become happier
We can change our paths and see what life has in store for us
Spring is the best possible time for any and all changes
Spring brings new lives
Spring brings the trees back to being colorful
Spring makes the world seem brighter
Spring brings us the sunny days
Spring brings back a gentle warmth
So when considering any sort of changes its best to choose Spring
It shows us a light
It shows us a better way
It shows us a more happier time
Spring can show you the things you may have forgotten about
Spring is the time of new blessings
So be blessed
Be happy
and become the best you that you can be
Look forward to the future and hold your head high

Escaped thoughts

I sometimes think I have a dragon
my dragon sits on my shoulder
He eats my thoughts
He eats the words I wish to speak
He makes me nervous and I stumble on my words
He makes me feel like a fool
He never lets me think straight
He only ever does as he pleases and interrupts my thoughts when I need to seriously think
In my most important moments he hits me with his tail and I lose my concentration
He will give me nightmares on pleasant nights
He will disturb my peace of mind with random things
He makes it hard to stay focused
This dragon does what he wants when he wants
He gives no warning
He never lets you go when he has you
He feeds on my misery
He feeds on my distraction
He makes me feel dreadful
Some days I defeat him
Most days he defeats me
That's when I get up, sharpen my sword, and try again
because some day I will beat him so bad he wont return

Days

Some days may be gray and sorrowful
Some days may be sunny and wonderful
Its on the days where the sun disappears, that we tend to be grumpy
Its those dark and dreary days
Where one thinks it might rain or it might storm
Where the sun has yet to be seen the entire day
Its on those days that I remember the true beauty of nature
Even on those dismal days
The green leaves against the dark sky, become brighter
So when you are having a dark day within yourself
Remember the green leaves
Remember that you aren't alone
Remember your friends and talk with them
Its on our darkest of days that we find out who are real friends are
They bring you joy
They make you laugh
They talk to you for a while
They make you think of the fun times
They make you think of the sun
They remind you that the darkness will pass
so when you are truly down and cant get up
when you do not have friends you can rely on
think of the sprouts growing on the trees
Do not wallow in pity
Do not remain sad
For the sun will come again soon
Things will always get better, as long as that is what you wish

No Matter

We work ourselves to the bone
We try so hard
We get hurt
We become overworked
We get bullied by coworkers
And for what?
To almost kill ourselves
To being told we are not good enough
To being told we need to do more
In the end what I have learned is that it does not matter
No matter how hard I work
No matter how many hours I put in
No matter how many bones I break
No matter perfect I do my job
No matter how helpful I am
No matter how nice I am
No matter what I do
It will never be enough
So instead of killing yourself for worthless people
Instead of beating yourself up
Instead of losing your confidence
Instead of losing your shine
Instead of remaining in a position where you go unappreciated
Leave that job
Leave those people
because if you remain, you only have yourself to blame

Bustling City

A sunny day in a large town
The large crowd makes me think everyone is downtown
They go shopping
They go drinking
They stop some place to have a small snack
They enjoy their afternoon in the sun
They go to their favorite Cafe
Some are energetic and happy
Others are stressed and frustrated
In all the years I have watched people pass me by
I have noticed something they all have in common
Almost everyone is happier when the sun is shining
You will hear people laughing
You will see people eating and enjoying every second of sun they can get
Germany has more rainy days then sunny
And so the people love the sun more than most
Most everyone is stressed from their day to day lives
But in these few minutes, they forget about it all
So my advice to all
Become someones sun, when they seem down
Do not let others dictate how great your day is
Do not let others pull you down just because they are not happy
Help them to have a better day
Because when you help someone else
Your day just gets that much better
Believe in yourself
Remain awesome but wholesome

Learn for the Future

The past is there for us to learn
It teaches us what we should not do
It is suppose to be a means to become better
As I sit alone a thought dawns upon me
Humans have not yet learned from the past
We still have mindless wars
We still have hate
We still have prejudice
Nothing has changed
Nothing ever will unless we make a stand
We must become courageous
We must stand up to others
We must stop these pointless wars
We must stop the pointless Hate
Because if we do not, and remain as we are
The world will have no future
The world will be lost to its demons
The world will become a black place
Humans will remain ignorant
They will forever be a problem
Unless we start changing
Unless we become smarter
Unless we stop being greedy
Unless we stop with pointless batter
Unless we stop being aggressive
nothing will change
The world will remain a dark and dismal place
It will forever be the last place most will wish to be